Star Singer

by Cathy West

Rans·m

StarStruck

Star Singer
by Cathy West

Illustrated by Gavin Campbell

Published by Ransom Publishing Ltd.
Radley House, 8 St. Cross Road, Winchester, Hants. SO23 9HX
www.ransom.co.uk

ISBN   978 184167 135 2

First published in 2014

Illustrations copyright © 2014 Gavin Campbell
Photographic images copyright ©: cover – Pali Rao; pages 4, 5 – Pali Rao; pages 6, 7 – 8213erika; D.S.B (http://www.flickr.com/people/16093955@N00); pages 8, 9 – Mykal Burns! http://www.flickr.com/photos /mykalburns/3616675960/); Nationaal Archief, Den Haag, Rijksfotoarchief: Fotocollectie Algemeen Nederlands Fotopersbureau (ANEFO) http://www.gahetna.nl/over-ons/open-datastu_spivack; William P. Gottlieb Collection (http://memory.loc.gov/ammem/wghtml/wghome.html); pages 10, 11 – gjp311; inspir8tion; Jason Meredith (http://www.flickr.com/people/74288833@N00); pages 12, 13 – Anna Omelchenko; Tsui; pages 14, 15 – Anest; Dephisticate (http://www.flickr.com/people/59622776@N05); Ayvan; goodynewshoes; pages 16, 17 – mattbuck (http://www.flickr.com/photos/mattbuck007/ 4398015003/); Rebbeck_Images; Achim Raschka/CC-BY-SA-3.0 (//commons.wikimedia.org/wiki/File:13-06-09_RaR_Dizzee _Rascal_17.jpg); black satin, passim – Jon Helgason.

A CIP catalogue record of this book is available from the British Library.

Contents

3

All About Being a Star Singer

What is a star singer?

Most people think star singers need to sing pop music.

But not always!

Most kinds of music have star singers. Here are some:

Jazz

Ella Fitzgerald
Billie Holiday

Pop music

Christina Aguilera
Michael Jackson

Classical music

Placido Domingo
Luciano Pavarotti

Country music

Dolly Parton
Johnny Cash

Reggae

Bob Marley
Jimmy Cliff

Rock

Freddie Mercury
Robert Plant

Some singers write their own songs. But many singers sing songs written by other people.

A star singer works with a **manager**. The manager runs their **business** for them. This helps the singer **focus** on the music.

 In a **recording studio** a **producer** will help the singer to get the right sound.

Star singer **Christina Aguilera**. She has sold over 50 million records around the world.

Billie Holiday (1915 - 1959). Her real name was Eleanora Fagan. She was also known as 'Lady Day'. Billie Holiday was a very important jazz singer.

Tom Jones. Born in South Wales, UK. First hit single 1965. Over 100 million albums sold. Now aged over 70, he is still making records.

Frank Sinatra. First album: 1946. He has sold more than 150 million records worldwide.

Édith Piaf (1915 - 1963). She sang in French, but was famous all over the world.

Elvis Presley. 'The King of Rock and Roll.' The best-selling solo artist of all time: he sold over 600 million albums.

9

Life as a star singer

What do star singers do all day?

- They **practise** (exercise their voice).

- They **rehearse** for concerts and albums.

- They work in **recording studios**, making albums.

- They do **interviews**.

- They travel a lot.

Life as a star singer can be hard.

You can earn a lot of money, but you can be away from home for a long time.

There's a lot of **pressure**, too.

- You can't have a bad day: your **audience** always wants a great **performance**.

- Everywhere you go, people may **recognise** you.

How to become a star singer

How do you become a star singer?

- ⭐ You need talent. You need to be a good singer.

- ⭐ You need to practise. Many famous singers practise every day.

- ⭐ Look after your voice. It's your instrument.

- ⭐ You need to get experience. Why not join a local band?

- ⭐ Listen to other singers. Learn from them.

- ⭐ Use YouTube and social media to get yourself known.

Many great singers never become stars.

You need to sing well. But you need to look like a star, too.

And you need to be lucky!

Simphiwe Dana. A star singer from South Africa.

Reality TV shows to find a star singer are very popular.

A singer can quickly become famous.

Is this the only way to become a star singer?

Carrie Underwood won the American Idol TV show in 2005. She is now a huge star.

Carrie has won six Grammy Awards. She is also a crossover star. Her records top the pop charts and the country music charts.

Winning a TV show makes you famous. But are you ready to be a star? Do you have the skills?

- Most singers start their **career** slowly.

- They learn how to be better singers.

- They learn how to put on good **concerts**.

- They learn how to work in a **recording studio**.

- They learn how to do **interviews**.

They do all this *before* they become famous.

When they become stars – they are ready.

15

Many singers are famous for just a few years. Then they are forgotten.

A *real* star will be famous for a long time.

Hip hop singer and rapper
Dizzee Rascal.

Do you *really* want to be a star?

- The press can be very nasty about famous people.

- You will need to behave like a star – all the time!

- Most great singers just want to sing. They don't 'want' to be a star. It just happened that way.

The Star Singer

Chapter One

Wrong image

Susan Straw sang like an angel. She had been chosen to sing at the grand opening of the new Super Mall.

Lucy was not happy.

'Why can't I be the star singer at the grand opening?' she whined to her dad.

Her dad was Tim Turner, the rich owner of the Super Mall.

'I didn't choose Susan Straw,' Mr Turner told his spoilt daughter.

Lucy stamped her foot.

Tim Turner owns the Super Mall. It's the grand opening.
Why can't I be the star singer?
I didn't choose Susan Straw!
Susan Straw sings like an angel.

Tim Turner's secretary, Claire, knocked at the door of his office.

'Susan Straw is here to meet you, Mr Turner,' Claire said.

She showed Susan in to the office.

Tim Turner looked at Susan. This was not the image he wanted for his Super Mall.

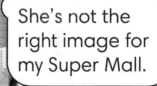

Chapter Two

'It's not fair'

As soon as Susan left the office, Lucy started nagging her dad again.

Claire watched in despair as Lucy tried to get her own way.

'It's not fair!' Lucy said. '*I* should be the star singer.'

Tim Turner sighed.

'OK, you're right!' he said. 'You *are* the right image for the Super Mall. You can sing at the grand opening.'

Lucy was over the moon. She was going to be the star singer at the grand opening, just like she wanted.

She gave her dad a hug.

'But what are we going to tell Susan?' Claire asked.

'You'll think of something,' Mr Turner said.

Chapter Three

'Your daughter can't sing'

A few days later, Claire spoke to her boss.

'Your daughter can't sing,' Claire said. 'She may look like a star, but she hasn't got the voice.'

Tim Turner scratched his head. He knew Claire was right. His daughter's singing was like fingernails scraping down an old chalk board.

'Get Susan Straw to sing backstage,' he said. 'Nobody will know it's not my daughter singing.'

Claire called Susan on the telephone.

She told Susan that she would be singing after all. But she would be hidden away backstage. Lucy would sing onstage and Susan's voice would be heard over the loudspeakers.

'It's still an honour to be chosen,' Susan said.

'It's not fair!' Claire thought to herself. 'They should see Susan *and* hear her. She is the star singer.'

Chapter Four

The big day

It was the big day. The day of the grand opening.

Lucy stood on stage in front of the microphone. She sang in time to the sound of Susan singing backstage.

Claire was watching Susan. Claire could see tears running down Susan's cheeks as she sang.

'This is wrong!' Claire thought. 'It's not fair. Susan should not be hidden away, just because she's not the right image for the Super Mall.'

Then Claire had an idea.

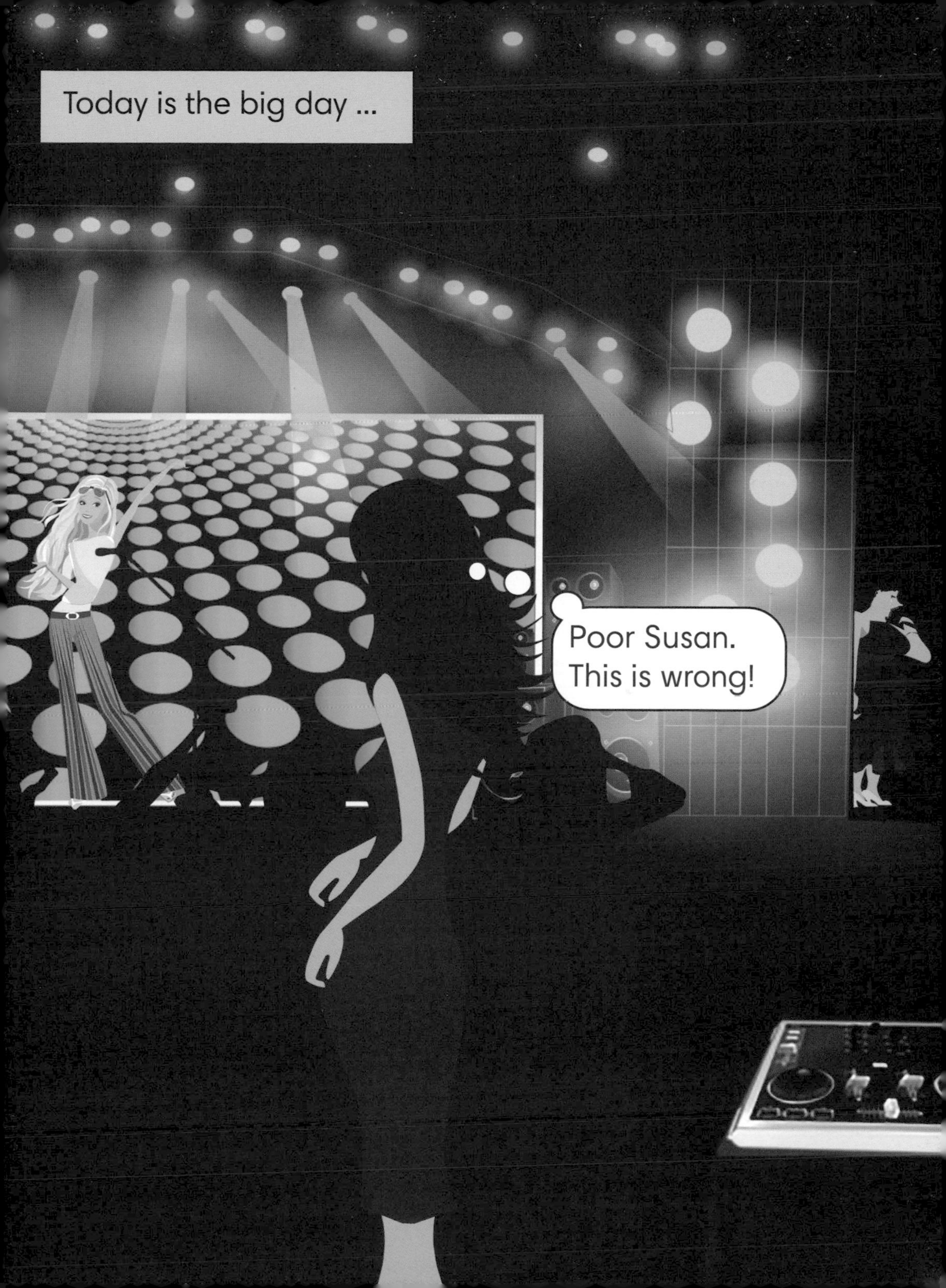
Today is the big day ...
Poor Susan. This is wrong!

Claire turned off Susan's microphone and quickly turned on Lucy's microphone.

Now everybody could hear Lucy singing out of tune.

People started to chant for the real star singer. Claire led the chant.

'We want the real singer! We want the real singer!'

Lucy stamped her foot and ran off stage to her dad.

Susan Straw walked on stage. Everyone cheered. Susan stood in front of the microphone and carried on singing. She sang like an angel.

Now everybody could see Susan and hear her. *She* was the star singer.

Curtain Call

audience	microphone
backstage	performance
business	practise
career	pressure
classical	producer
country	reality TV
experience	recognise
famous	recording studio
focus	reggae
instrument	rehearse
interview	secretary
jazz	social media
manager	talent